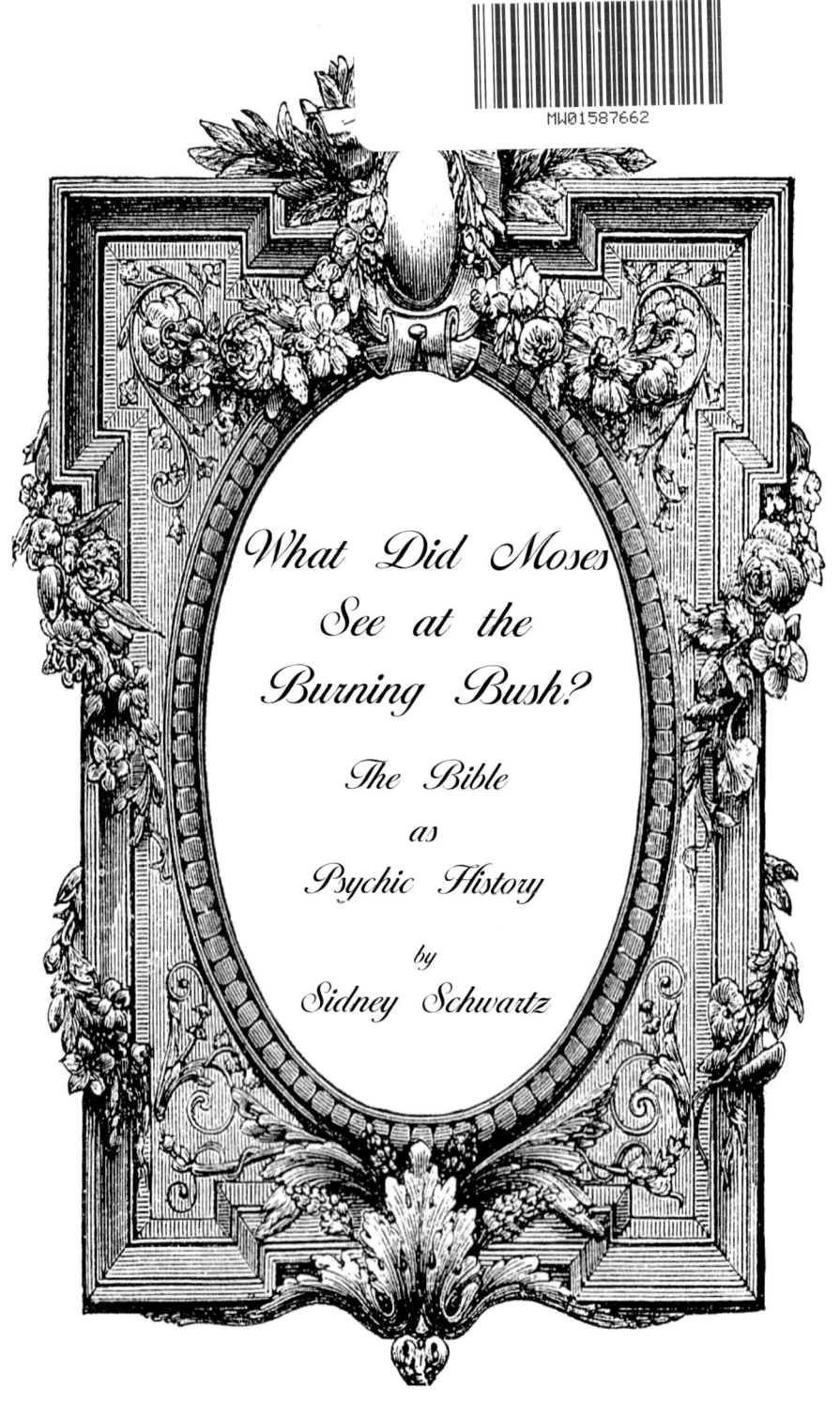

What Did Moses See at the Burning Bush?

The Bible as Psychic History

by
Sidney Schwartz

What Did Moses See at the Burning Bush?
The Bible as Psychic History
Volume 7

by Sidney Schwartz

Copyright © 2015 Gifts of the Spirit Church, Inc.
First Edition
Published in 2015.

All rights reserved. No part of this book may be reproduced, stored in a mechanical retrieval system or transmitted in any form by electronic, video, laser, mechanical, photocopying, recording means or otherwise, in part or in whole, without written consent of the publisher.

ISBN# 978-1519539885
Printed in the U.S.A.

	Bible as Psychic History Series
Volume 1	Overview
Volume 2	You Can't See the Forest from the Trees
Volume 3	Adam & Eve: The Suppression of Women
Volume 4	How Did Abraham See God?

WHAT DID MOSES SEE AT THE BURNING BUSH?

Often people have questioned how was Moses able to see flames burning a bush, but the wood of the bush remained intact? The answer to this question is easily answered through psychic science.

Moses did **NOT** see a bush burning with his physical eyes. Instead Moses had his first clairvoyant vision; he saw a bush "on fire" in "his mind's eye."

When our eyes capture an image, that image travels through the optic nerve to a center in our brain, which interprets the signal, and then we "see" the image. When a clairvoyant sees a clairvoyant vision, which is captured by the "psychic eyes" or the eyes of the etheric (spirit) body, it then travels to a different brain center that specializes in interpreting clairvoyant visions. This center has atrophied in most people's brains, and is only active in people who have developed the *Gift of Clairvoyance*.

At the Burning Bush, Moses saw *Spirit Lights* that appeared to be a burning fire, but would not have heat or flame. Spirit created this "fire" in the Spirit World; therefore, "the flames" would vibrate on a much too high a frequency to be able to burn physical wood.

Another interesting question is: Did Moses see God in the Burning Bush? Or did he just see flames? We must rely on the Bible for the answers to these questions.

> **There the angel of the LORD appeared to him *as* a flame coming from the middle of a bush. Moses saw that the bush was on fire but that it was not burning up.**[1]

---

[1] Exodus 3:2 [TEV].

As is often the case, Bible translators do not agree on how to word their English translations. The **ASV** Bible translates this same verse as:

> **And the angel of Jehovah appeared unto him *in* a flame of fire out of the midst of a bush: and he looked, and, behold, the bush burned with fire, and the bush was not consumed.**[2]

There are other translations that provide us with additional information; however; their sources are not identified, and their accuracy may be questionable. **ETHJ** is the only Old Testament of the 244 I have studied, to reveal the name of the angel, speaking at the Burning Bush, as *Zagnugael.*[3] **BATE** claims the Burning Bush was actually a *palm tree.*[4] **ABDNT** says: *"And there appeared to him the angel of the Lord through the waves of fire from inside the sun disc."*[5]

The **ASV** and **TEV** translations paint radically different pictures. As we visualize **TEV**'s phrase *"as a flame,"* we see Moses watching the burning flames, and then Moses heard the angel of the Lord's voice. However, in **ASV**'s picture of Moses sees the angel of God, surrounded by flames. Which of these pictures is more accurate? We can answer that question by studying the original Hebrew.

When we examine this verse using *The Interlinear Hebrew-English Old Testament,* a book which translates Hebrew words into English, word by word, we find the Hebrew phrase בְּלַבַּת־אֵשׁ is translated as:

---

[2] Exodus 3:2 [ASV].
[3] Exodus 3:2 [ETHJ].
[4] Exodus 3:2 [BATE].
[5] Exodus 3:2 [ABDNT].

What Did Moses See at the Burning Bush?   3

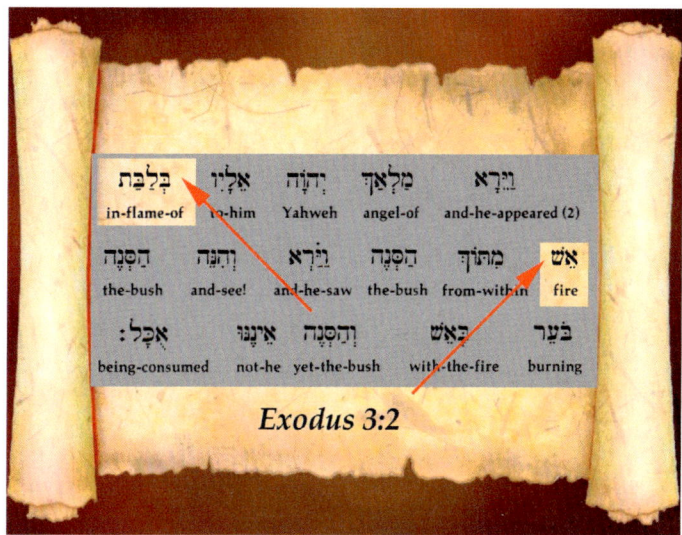

Exodus 3:2

"in-flame-of fire."[6] (Please note Hebrew is read from the right side of the page to the left.)

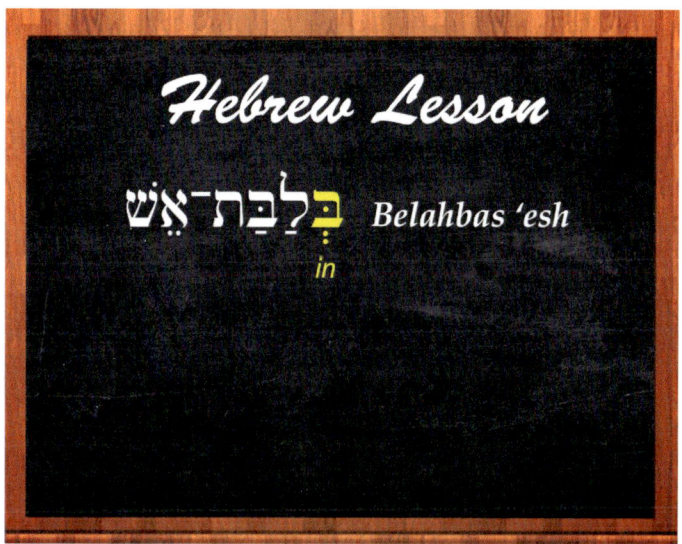

In the word בְּלַבַּת the first letter בְּ is a prefix, which means *in*. Therefore, the ASV is a more literal translation of the original Hebrew.[7]

---

[6] Kohlenberger, John R., III. *The NIV Interlinear Hebrew-English Old Testament. Vol. 1. Genesis – Deuteronomy.* Grand Rapids, MI: Zondervan, 1980. p. 150.

From examining the Hebrew, it would appear that Moses **did** see *the angel of the Lord.*

However, we are still left with the same question: Did Moses see God, himself, in the Burning Bush? It is my opinion Moses did **not** see God, but only the flames of the Burning Bush.

I have often questioned why the story of the Burning Bush begins with *an Angel of the Lord* speaking to Moses.

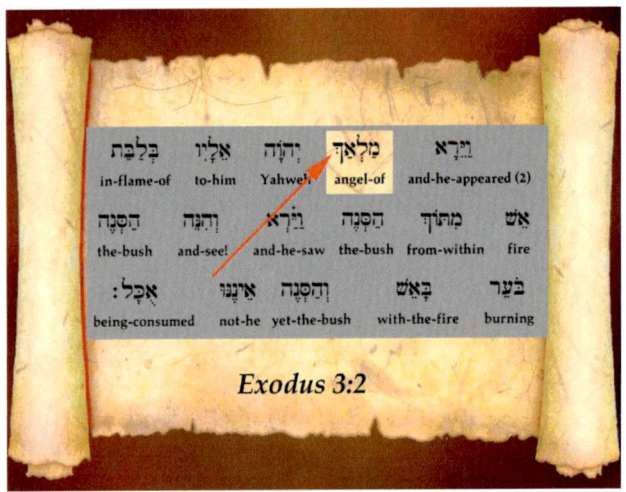

Exodus 3:2

The Interlinear Hebrew-English Old Testament, uses the Hebrew word מַלְאַךְ/*mal'ak* that is translated as *angel*; however, *The Englishman's Hebrew and Chaldee Concordance* translates מַלְאַךְ/*mal'ak* as **messenger.**[8]

However, by verse 4, suddenly, and inexplicably **God** is conversing with Moses.

---

[7] "Judaism 101: Hebrew Language: Root Words." *Judaism 101: Hebrew Language: Root Words.* N.p., n.d. Web. 24 Nov. 2015. <http://www.jewfaq.org/root.htm>.

[8] *The Englishman's Hebrew and Chaldee Concordance of the Old Testament.* Vol. 1. London: Walton and Maberrly, 1866. p. 704.

What Did Moses See at the Burning Bush?

> **When the LORD saw that he had gone over to look, God called to him from within the bush, "Moses! Moses!" And Moses said, "Here I am."**[9]

What would account for this change of speaker? Recently, the answer to this question flashed through my mind. It happened because of a gap in vibration or frequency. Communication between a human medium and a spirit person can only take place when the Spirit lowers its frequency, and the medium raises his/her frequency, and the two meet in the middle, on the exact same frequency (or vibration).

When Moses was a young man he witnessed a taskmaster beating a Hebrew. This enraged Moses, and blinded by his anger, Moses killed the Egyptian. Then Moses feared punishment for his crime, and fled Egypt.

Moses traveled and settled in the land of Midian, where he became a shepherd. The job of a shepherd required him to spend much time alone, to make sure the sheep grazed properly, and did not wander away from the flock. In his solitude, Moses naturally began to meditate. He learned to quiet his mind and body, allowing his thoughts to go deep within. He then listened to the consciousness within his soul or etheric body. Therefore, Moses naturally developed the mediumistic gifts of clairaudience (begin able to hear Spirit's voice) and clairvoyance (being able to see Spirit).

When Moses came upon the Burning Bush, he had his first mediumistic experience; this was the very first time Moses could see and hear Spirit.

It is important to understand there are 6 levels or dimensions in the Spirit World, which most people call heaven.

---

[9] Exodus 3:4 [NIV].

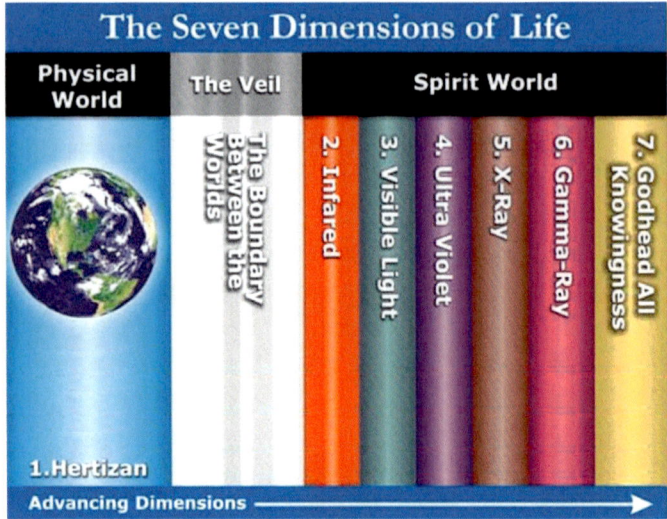

This illustration represents the six levels of the Spirit World. When you read the level's names, as the number of the level increases so does the vibration or frequency.

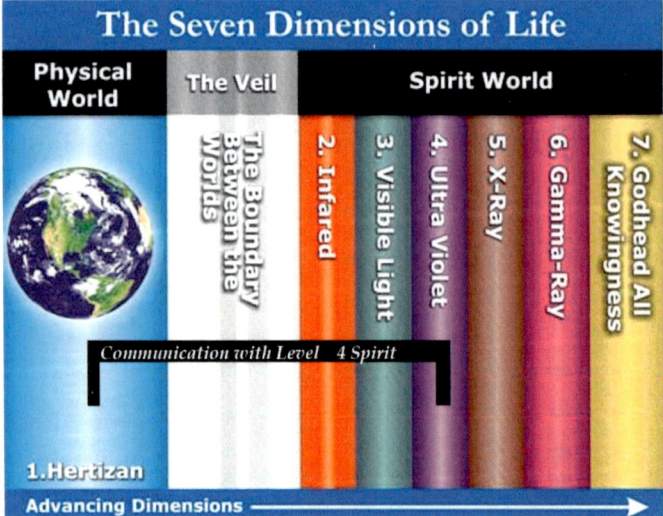

The black bar in this illustration shows communication between a medium living in the physical or Hertizan level and a level 4 Spirit.

What Did Moses See at the Burning Bush? 7

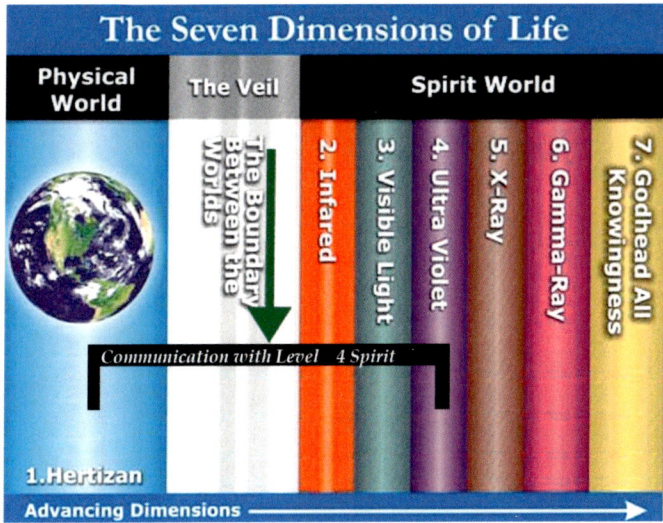

The green arrow represents the meeting point where the communication link is established between the medium and the level 4 Spirit.

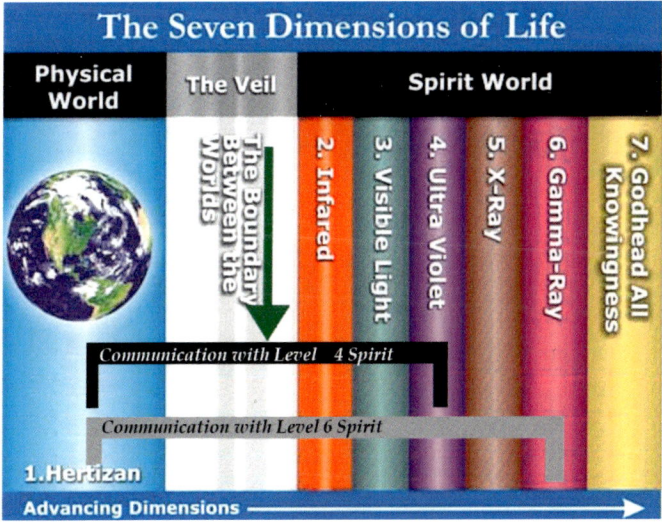

The grey bar shows communication between a medium and a Spirit living on the 6th level.

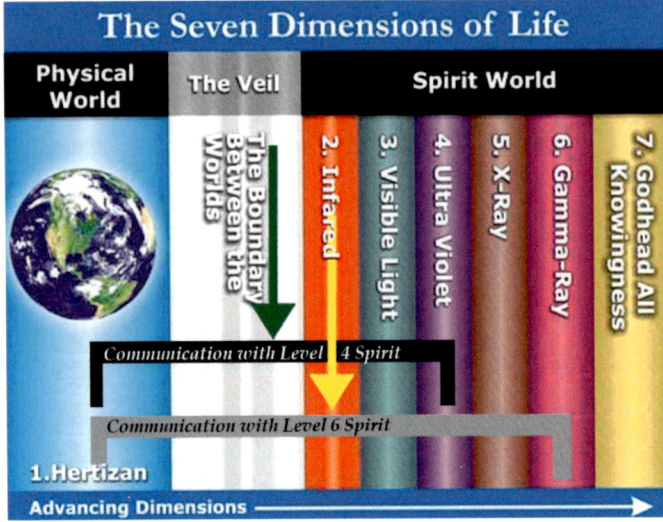

The yellow arrow represents the meeting point where the communication link is established between the medium and the level 6 Spirit.

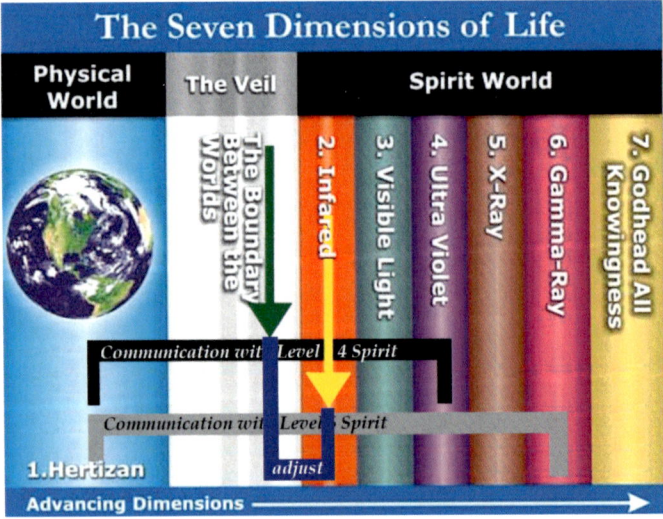

Notice how much higher a medium has to adjust his frequency to communicate with the level 6 Spirit than the level 4 Spirit.

It is important to understand the purpose of the different levels in the Spirit World — levels of spiritual progression, advancement, and growth. A soul will gravitate naturally to the level that was earned during its physical life. For example, if the person committed bad deeds, or lived a life of crime, then upon death that soul arrives on one of the lowest levels of the Spirit World. Spirits from the higher levels, would descended to the lower levels to teach or council the Spirits residing there. When a soul advances in enlightenment, it earns the right to move up to the next higher level in the Spirit World.

This concept has a Biblical basis, which is found in Genesis chapter 28 verses 10-15 in the story of the dream of Jacob's ladder.

> **Jacob left Beersheba and set out for Haran. When he reached a certain place, he stopped for the night because the sun had set. Taking one of the stones there, he put it under his head and lay down to sleep.**
>
> **He had a dream in which he saw a stairway resting on the earth, with its top reaching to heaven, and the angels of God were ascending and descending on it.**[10]

The KJV uses the word *ladder* instead of *stairway*, in this verse.

This is the reason the Bible states: *"and the angels of God were ascending and descending on it."*[11] The path of spiritual progress is never closed, and there is no known end to the advancement of the individual. All Spirits have the opportunity to advance during their life in the Spirit World, to become more enlightened beings.

---

[10] Genesis 28:10-12 [NIV].
[11] Genesis 28:12 [NIV].

We can safely assume when Moses communicated with "the Lord" the Spirit resided on level 6 or 7, on the highest levels of the Spirit World.

Jesus taught us the words *God* and *Spirit* are interchangeable. We learn this when we read the story of Jesus giving the Samaritan Woman a reading as they were sitting by Jacob's well (John 4:24).

> *God* is *spirit*, and his worshipers must worship in the Spirit and in truth.[12]

Truthfully, this verse is **NOT** exactly what Jesus said. Translators have taken the liberty of interchanging the word *God* and *Spirit* from the original Greek wording.

John 4:24 [Tischendorf's 1872]

Of the 404 New Testaments I have studied, only 2 versions have literally translated the original Greek, by placing the word *Spirit* before the word *God*.

---

[12] John 4:24 [NIV].

In **[HORNS]** George Horner's *Coptic Version of the New Testament Vol. 3* published by Clarendon Press in 1911, John 4:24 reads:

> A *spirit* is *God*; and for those who will worship him it is right for them to worship him in spirit and truth.[13]

Glenn David Bauscher's The Original Aramaic New Testament in Plain English: An American Translation of the Aramaic New Testament. 3rd edition, published in 2009. **[OANT]** John 4:24 reads:

> For The *Spirit* is *God*, and it is fitting that those who worship him worship in The Spirit and in The Truth.[14]

Since the human mind interprets language visually, when we read "*God* is *Spirit*" most people visualize an old man with a long grey beard sitting on a throne up in heaven watching over all of humankind, that morphs into Casper the friendly ghost.

When we read: "*Spirit is God*" we visualize Casper the friendly ghost morphing into the old man sitting on his heavenly throne. Therefore, there is consequence to the word placement. I believe Bible translators deliberately rearranged the words in order to focus Bible readers' attention on "the old man sitting on his heavenly throne."

In Biblical times, people were very class conscious. A servant would always call his or her master "*my Lord*," or "*my Lordship*." People, who spoke with Spirit, who most people could not see, referred to the entity living on a higher frequency as ***the Lord***, as a sign of respect.

---

[13] John 4:24 [HORNS].
[14] John 4:24 [OANT].

In the Hebrew Old Testament, God has 20 different names. In most cases, Bible translators translate *all these different names* with the singular phrase: "the Lord."

NAMES OF GOD

#	Name of God	Translation	Bible Verse
1	ELOAH	God "mighty, strong, prominent"	(Genesis 7:1 Isaiah 9:6)
2	EL	"power"	(Genesis 31:29)
3	ELOHIM	God "Creator, Mighty and Strong"	(Genesis 17:7 Jeremiah 31:33)
4	EL SHADDAI	"God Almighty," "The Mighty One of Jacob"	(Genesis 49:24 Psalm 132:2,5)
5	ADONAI	"Lord"	(Genesis 15:2 Judges 6:15)
6	YHWH / YAHWEH / JEHOVAH	"LORD"	(Deuteronomy 6:4 Daniel 9:14)
7	YAHWEH-JIREH	"The Lord Will Provide"	(Genesis 22:14)
8	YAHWEH- RAPHA	"The Lord Who Heals"	(Exodus 15:26)
9	YAHWEH-NISSI	"The Lord Our Banner"	(Exodus 17:15)
10	YAHWEH-M'KADDESH	"The Lord Who Sanctifies, Makes Holy"	(Leviticus 20:8 Ezekiel 37:28)
11	YAHWEH-SHALOM	"The Lord Our Peace"	(Judges 6:24)
12	YAHWEH-ELOHIM	"LORD God"	(Genesis 2:4 Psalm 59:5)
13	YAHWEH-TSIDKENU	"The Lord Our Righteousness"	(Jeremiah 33:16)
14	YAHWEH-ROHI	"The Lord Our Shepherd"	(Psalm 23:1)
15	YAHWEH-SHAMMAH	"The Lord Is There"	(Ezekiel 48:35)
16	YAHWEH-SABAOTH	"The Lord of Hosts"	(Isaiah 1:24 Psalm 46:7)
17	.EL ELYON	"Most High"	(Deuteronomy 26:19)
18	EL ROI	"God of Seeing"	(Genesis 16:13)
19	EL-OLAM	"Everlasting God"	(Psalm 90:1-3)
20	EL-GIBHOR	"Mighty God"	(Isaiah 9:6)

Returning to our discussion of Spirit communication with different level spirits, we must remember the Burning Bush was Moses first mediumistic experience. Therefore, in all likelihood, a lower level spirit, a *messenger* or *angel* of the Lord, a level 4 Spirit began the communication.

What Did Moses See at the Burning Bush?

Again Spirit was not confident Moses would even receive their message. This is clearly stated in Exodus 3:4.

> **When the LORD saw that he had caught Moses' attention, God called to him from the bush, "Moses! Moses!" "Here I am!" Moses replied.**[15]

Once Moses responded, then the Lord began his important discussion with Moses.

As Moses spoke with this level 4 Spirit, *the Angel of the Lord*, the Spirit doctors and chemists adjusted Moses' frequency to a higher level, until it reached the meeting point of the level 6 Spirit. Then direct communication with *the Lord* commenced.

This is **NOT** just a theory. I experienced this same process with Rev. Carl R. Hewitt when he began to channel Awan, the Angel Without a Name, and we began working on "the Encounter Books."[16]

For the first 20 or 25 trance sessions, a Spirit named Nathaniel was the first to speak. He would just chat with me for a few minutes, explaining the medium, Rev. Hewitt, could not bring Awan through at that point. Carl's frequency was not yet high enough to connect with Awan. The Spirit chemists adjusted Carl's frequency while Nathaniel chatted away. Then suddenly, Nathaniel announced he was stepping back to allow another Spirit to use the medium. It was then Awan would greet me, and our intense conversations began. After about 25 sessions, Carl must have learned to adjust directly to Awan's frequency, and Nathaniel no longer needed to speak first to "warm up" the medium.

After discussing the original Hebrew we are still left with the question did Moses see God (as a human being) in

---

[15] Exodus 3:4 [NLT].
[16] See pages 36-38.

the Burning Bush as Raphael depicted in the loggia in the Vatican?

This picture of God speaking with Moses at the Burning Bush is part of Raphael's Loggia at the Vatican.[17]

The famous artist Raphael, whose full name was Raffaello Sanzio da Urbino, (1483 –1520) was an Italian painter and architect of the High Renaissance. [18]

> **He also designed and painted the *Loggia* at the Vatican, a long thin gallery then open to a courtyard on one side....**[19]

Or did Moses just see the flames of the Burning Bush, and heard the voice of the *angel* and then *the Lord*?

---

[17] "Loggia Di Raffaello: 25 - 30." *Loggia Di Raffaello: 25 - 30*. N.p., n.d. Web. 24 Nov. 2015. <http://www.christusrex.org/www1/stanzas/L30b-Bush.jpg>.
[18] "Raphael." *Wikipedia*. Wikimedia Foundation, n.d. Web. 24 Nov. 2015. <https://en.wikipedia.org/wiki/Raphael>.
[19] "Raphael." *Wikipedia*. Wikimedia Foundation, n.d. Web. 24 Nov. 2015. <https://en.wikipedia.org/wiki/Raphael>.

What Did Moses See at the Burning Bush?

I would theorize that Moses saw the angel, because it was a lower level messenger; however, Moses only saw flames when *The Lord* spoke to him. I base this opinion on the original Hebrew wording. In Exodus 4:2 we found the prefix for the word *in*, attached to the word *flames*. Then we are told Moses saw the flames of the bush, which drew his attention and made him curious, in Exodus 4:4.

However I find more compelling evidence in Exodus chapter 33, which indicates that Moses became fixated on seeing God. We are told: "Moses saw God face to face as a man sees his friend" inside the Meeting Tent.[20]

To understand how Moses saw God face to face, one has to understand the rare *Gift of Materialization,* which is the "appearance of temporary solidification of ectoplasm."[21] We find the definition of *ectoplasm* in *The Encyclopedia of Occultism & Parapsychology*:

> "... a mysterious vapor like substance that ... streamed out of the body of entranced mediums."[22]

The *Prairie Ghosts* website enhances our understanding, when it states *ectoplasm* is:

> ... a combination of substances from both the physical and Spirit Worlds, and has a whitish to grayish smoky appearance, that comes through orifices (mouth, nostril, ears, etc.) of the medium.[23]

---

[20] Exodus 33:11.
[21] Blunsdon, Norman. *A Popular Dictionary of Spiritualism.* NY: Citadel Press, 1963. p. 128.
[22] Melton, J. Gordon, ed. *Encyclopedia of Occultism & Parapsychology.* 5th edition. Vol. 1. Detroit, MI: Gale Research Co., 2001. p. 469.
[23] Taylor, Troy. "ECTOPLASM Was this Mysterious Substance Fraud or Phantasm?" Haunted Museum. Accessed July 16, 2011.
http://www.prairieghosts.com/ectoplasm.html.

Under the correct conditions, Spirit withdraws ectoplasm from the cells of the medium's body and utilizes a type of life force energy that emanates from the ectoplasm. Ectoplasm looks like a whitish cloudy substance, especially when it first exits the medium's body.

Ectoplasm is very sensitive to light, therefore, materialization séances usually occur in complete darkness, or lit with red light. If white lights were turned on during the séance, it would destroy the ectoplasm, thus ending all communication. This sudden shock would be very hazardous, and even fatal to the medium. Under very special conditions, which Spirit determines, ectoplasm may be produced in daylight, but this is very rare.

In order to demonstrate the *Gift of Materialization*, the medium usually sits in a cabinet, which is an enclosed space, such as a small closet. The cabinet is usually curtained, to create a small area of total darkness. Next ectoplasm is withdrawn from the medium's body, through an orifice. Then Spirit mixes other chemicals and spiritual energy into the ectoplasm, which makes it sensitive to thought. Now Spirit people use thought energy to mold or form images of their faces, or even a fully formed replica of their physical bodies, which can talk and have a conversation with their loved ones. This provides irrefutable evidence to prove their identities, and validates their spirits continue to live in another higher dimension.

As with almost all aspects of psychic science, we find evidence the Hebrews used a cabinet to communicate with Spirit or God. In the book of Exodus chapters 25 and 26 we read of detailed instructions on how to build the **holy of holies** inside the tabernacle, the tent of God, which was actually a medium's cabinet.

> "And you shall hang the veil from the clasps, and bring the ark of the testimony in thither within the veil; and the veil shall separate for you the holy place from the

What Did Moses See at the Burning Bush?

most holy."[24]

Exodus chapter 25 verse 22 reads:

> "And there I will meet with you; and from above the mercy seat, from between the two cherubim which are upon the ark of the testimony, I will speak to you about all that I will give you in commandment for the sons of Israel."[25]

God's instructions were to build the **Holy of Holies**, a smaller, curtained sanctuary at the far end of the tabernacle. This was to create a small enclosure, to serve as a permanent cabinet, where God could materialize and speak to Moses "face to face," and provide guidance on how to lead the people.

We read regular materialization séances were held as the Hebrew traveled in the desert on their journey to the Promised Land. The first half of Exodus Chapter 33 verse 7 reads:

> Now Moses used to take the tent and pitch it outside the camp, a good distance from the camp, and he called it the *tent of meeting*.[26]

When we consult The Interlinear Hebrew-English Old Testament, we find the phrase אֹהֶל מוֹעֵד/*'ō·hel mō·w·'êḏ*, which is translated as *tent of meeting*.[27] However, *The Englishman's Hebrew and Chaldee Concordance of the Old*

---

[24] Exodus 26:33 [RSV].
[25] Exodus 25:22 [NASB].
[26] Exodus 33:7a [RSV].
[27] Kohlenberger, John R., III. *The NIV Interlinear Hebrew-English Old Testament. Vol. 1. Genesis – Deuteronomy.* Grand Rapids, MI: Zondervan, 1980. p. 241.

Testament translates the phrase differently, אֹהֶל/'ō·hel is translated as *tent*, and מוֹעֵד/mō·w·'êḏ as *appointed time*.[28]

The psychic relevance of the Hebrew word מוֹעֵד/mō·w·'êḏ translated as *appointed time*, is very significant. Moses consulted God, on a regular basis, seeking guidance on how best to lead the Hebrews. It was extremely important for Moses, just as it is still important for today's mediums, to establish an appointment with Spirit. Often a Spirit works with several mediums, and cannot always come on demand; therefore, appointments help Spirit to establish their schedule. This further proves materialization séances were being held on a regular basis.

When comparing the wording of Exodus 33:7 we discover Bible translators have created a list of 44 different terms to translate the Hebrew phrase אֹהֶל מוֹעֵד/'ō·hel mō·w·'êḏ into English. ETHJ states אֹהֶל מוֹעֵד/'ō·hel mō·w·'êḏ or the cabinet was to be a *"House of Instruction,"* [29] and ARAON calls it *Tent of the house of study*.[30] Both are psychically accurate translations, since the cabinet was to be a hall of learning — a place for people to learn the will of God, and to study spiritual truths.

In the second half of Exodus chapter 33 verse 7 we discover the motivation for people going to the Meeting Tent:

> **And it came about, that everyone who sought the Lord would go out to the tent of meeting, which was outside the camp.**[31]

When we consult the original Hebrew we find the phrase מְבַקֵּשׁ יְהוָה/məḇaq·qêš Yah·weh, which translates as

---

[28] *The Englishman's Hebrew and Chaldee Concordance of the Old Testament.* Vol. 2. London: Walton and Maberrly, 1866. p. 1466 & 1653.
[29] Exodus 33:7a [ETHJ].
[30] Exodus 33:7a [ARAON].
[31] Exodus 33:7b [NASB].

What Did Moses See at the Burning Bush?

inquiring Yahweh.[32] However, once again Bible translators have created a list of 37 terms to translate מְבַקֵּשׁ יְהוָה/*məḇaq·qêš Yah·weh* into English.

The meaning of many of these translations is quite clear: people who wanted guidance or advice from God/Spirit would go to the Meeting Tent. These translations state this fact clearly:

COV	Ask any question at the Lord
GEDD	Consult the Lord
AEB	Wanted an answer from Jehovah

However, several Bibles severely alter this verse's meaning.

NIrV	Ask the Lord a question
OGD	Desiring to make his prayer to the Lord
ETHJ	Turned by repentance with a true heart before the Lord

Most people would agree there is a significant difference between asking the Lord a question, praying to him, or repenting. Why would Bible translators choose the words *pray* and *repent* rather than *question*? Do they want to disguise the fact one could receive an immediate answer from God/Spirit? Were the translators trying to hide the fact that in biblical times people were able to talk to God and receive an answer? Would people start to question why the ancient Hebrews could have a two-way conversation with God, while people living in the 21st century are told they cannot?

In biblical times, people who wanted guidance from Spirit, or as the Bible states: *"consult or inquire of God,"* went to the Meeting Tent. This opportunity existed for all the people, not just a special few. However, theologians representing orthodox religions sought to deny mankind the opportunity of this divine guidance, when they placed the

---

[32] Kohlenberger, John R., III. *The NIV Interlinear Hebrew-English Old Testament. Vol. 1. Genesis – Deuteronomy.* Grand Rapids, MI: Zondervan, 1980. p. 241.

psychically ungifted priest as the intermediary between God and the people instead of the true medium or prophet, as God had intended.

As we continue reading Exodus chapter 33, verses 8-11 describe a Spirit materialization séance.

> **And it came about, whenever Moses went out to the tent, that all the people would arise and stand, each at the entrance of his tent, and gaze after Moses until he entered the tent.**
>
> **And it came about, whenever Moses entered the tent, the pillar of cloud would descend and stand at the entrance of the tent; and the LORD would speak with Moses.**
>
> **When all the people saw the pillar of cloud standing at the entrance of the tent, all the people would arise and worship, each at the entrance of his tent.**[33]

When we examine the original Hebrew we find the phase עַמּוּד הֶעָנָן / *'am·mūḏ he·'ā·nān* translated as *pillar of the cloud*,[34] which is actually *ectoplasm*. This was the same cloudy substance that formed on Mount Sinai prior to the Hebrews hearing the Ten Commandments through trumpet mediumship.[35]

We continue reading the Bible with verse 11.

> **Inside the tent, the Lord spoke to Moses face to face, as a man speaks to his friend. Afterwards Moses would return to the camp, but the young man who assisted**

---

[33] Exodus 33:8-10 [NASB].
[34] Kohlenberger, John R., III. *The NIV Interlinear Hebrew-English Old Testament. Vol. 1. Genesis – Deuteronomy*. Grand Rapids, MI: Zondervan, 1980. p. 241.
[35] Exodus chapters 19-20.

What Did Moses See at the Burning Bush?

him, Joshua (son of nun) stayed behind in the tabernacle."[36]

The laws of psychic science have never changed. What was true in biblical times, can still happen today. This includes the *Gift of Materialization*.

In 1953, in Ephrata, Pennsylvania, a materialization séance took place where Jack Edwards photographed a spirit materialization with infrared film. Ethel Post-Parrish was the medium and Silver Belle was the Spirit who materialized at this séance.

The medium, Ethel Post-Parrish, sat in a cabinet, a small, enclosed space, and ectoplasm was withdrawn from her body. The spirit of Silver Belle molded this ectoplasm, which the Bible calls *a pillar of cloud*, into a replica of her physical body. Silver Bell created vocal cords in this ectoplasmic body, and spoke to the physical people who witnessed this séance.

In order to prove the validity of her special gift, Ethel Post Parrish invited parapsychologists and medical doctors, to witness the materialization phenomenon, and to run experiments, provided spirit gave its permission.

The pamphlet entitled: *"Lo I am with you Alway,"* quotes Charles Richet's *30 Years of Psychical Research*.

> "Professor Charles Richet in his book- "Thirty Years of Psychical Research," describes materialization as the production of a "being formed of living matter." He claims that these materialized forms have a circulation of blood and also respiration. He goes on to say that in his experiments he has found that the spirit form has a will and a personality entirely separate from that of the medium."[37]

---

[36] Exodus 33:11 [LIV].
[37] Jefts, Lena Barnes. *Lo, I Am With You Alway*. Casadaga, FL: National Spiritualist Churches, n. d. p. 36.

During one experimental materialization séance, Ethel Post Parrish sat on a scale. 37 pounds of ectoplasm was withdrawn from her body. When the séance concluded only 35 pounds returned to her body.[38] Where did the rest of it go? The spirit people used that energy during the process of molding and animating the ectoplasm into a replica of Silver Bell's physical body.

> ... the use of psychic force or energy is a drain upon the vitality of the medium. This is especially true when there are negative vibrations in the room.[39]

Through psychic research in the 20th century, it was proven the *Gift of Materialization* depletes the medium's energy more than any other **Gift of the Spirit**. Ethel Post Parrish was so exhausted after this séance, (from this loss of energy) that she couldn't move. The fact the Bible states: *"Joshua (son of nun) stayed behind in the tabernacle,"* proves he served as materialization medium, which allowed Moses to speak to God "face to face." This would be the only reason Joshua too tired to leave the Meeting Tent?

Therefore, it is curious why Moses was still not satisfied, and once again asked God to see his face. As we continue reading Exodus chapter 33 we find a record of this second request, which seems contradict Moses' face-to-face dialogue with God. However, our knowledge of psychic science will prove that a contradiction does not exist. Exodus 33:18-23 reads:

---

[38] Jefts, Lena Barnes. *Lo, I Am With You Alway*. Casadaga, FL: National Spiritualist Churches, n. d. p. 36-37.
[39] Jefts, Lena Barnes. *Lo, I Am With You Alway*. Casadaga, FL: National Spiritualist Churches, n. d. p. 37.

What Did Moses See at the Burning Bush?
Silver Belle Materialization Séance 1953
Ethel Post-Parrish, Medium — Jack Edwards, Infra-Red Photographer

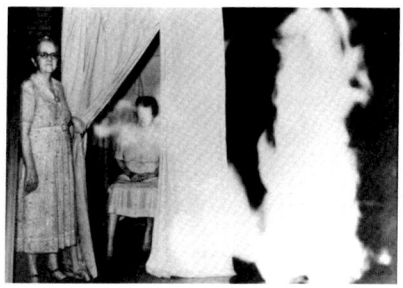

1. The white, smoky ectoplasm is drawn from medium, sitting inside of the cabinet.

2. The *Pillar of Cloud* coming from the medium's body forms from the ground upwards.

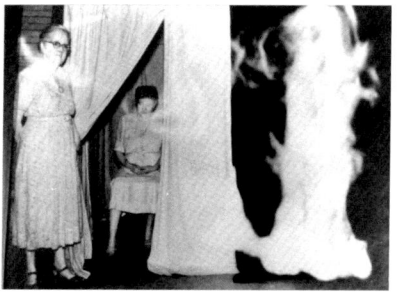

3. It is the thoughts of Silver Belle that molds the pillar of cloud.

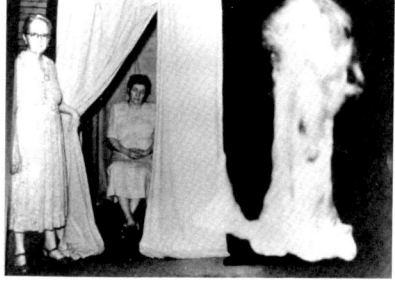

4. More of Silver Belle's features become visible in the column of ectoplasm.

5. Silver Belle can now speak to the people attending the séance.

6. Silver Belle blesses everyone, as her ectoplasmic form breaks up, retracting into the medium's body, Not all returns, the medium will be exhausted.

> "Then Moses said, I pray Thee, show me Thy glory!"
>
> "And He said, I Myself will make all My goodness pass before you, and will proclaim the name of the Lord before you; and I will be gracious to whom I will be gracious and will show compassion on whom I will show compassion."
>
> "But He said, You cannot see My face for no man can see Me and live!"[40]

This verse would raise several questions in the mind of someone ignorant of the *Gifts of the Spirit*, and the laws of psychic science. In Exodus 33:11 Moses is described as talking to God *"face to face, as a man speaks to his friend."* How it is possible to talk to someone face to face, *and yet not see that face?*

To one educated in the *Gifts of the Spirit*, there is no contradiction. Everyone attending the materialization séance is able to see the face of the Spirit, using one's physical eyes, since the face made of *ectoplasm,* a semi-physical substance, that vibrates on a frequency within the range of human sight. Just as everyone could see Silver Bell's face in the column of ectoplasm, Moses unmistakably saw the Lord's face.

When Moses asked to see God's glory, in Exodus 33:20, he was asking to see God's *etheric body*, or to say it another way, God's Spirit body or soul. When God said:

> "But He said, You cannot see My face for no man can see Me and live!"[41]

God told Moses the only way Moses could see His spiritual body would be to go through the transition of death. The Spirit people live in etheric bodies, which are bodies of energy. The etheric body of God, residing on the highest level

---

[40] Exodus 33:18-23 [NASB].
[41] Exodus 33:20 [NASB].

What Did Moses See at the Burning Bush?

of the Spirit World, would be far too bright, and its energy so intense that it would kill any human who looked at it.

This passage lends credence to my theory Moses did **not** see God in the Burning Bush, because Moses still desired to see God directly.

WHY IS MOSES DEPICTED WITH HORNS?

Many artists including Michelangelo portrayed Moses with horns on his forehead. What was the origin of this concept? The answer is found in psychic science and the mistranslation of a Hebrew word in the Bible's text.

Chapter 34 of Exodus verses 27-29 reads:

> "Then the Lord said to Moses write down these words for in accordance with them I have made a covenant with you and with Israel. So Moses stayed there with the Lord for forty days and forty nights without eating any food, or drinking any water, and he wrote on the tablets the words of the covenant the Ten Commandments. As Moses came down from Mount Sinai with the two tablets of the commandments in his hands he did not know that the skin in *his face had become radiant* while he conversed with the Lord."[42]

Moses spent a very long period of 40 days and nights in God's presence. If Moses had seen God's face, during this experience, I am confident it would be mentioned in the Bible. Yet, being in God's presence for such a long time did affect Moses' physical body.

When we consult *The Interlinear Hebrew-English Old Testament*, we find the Hebrew word קָרַן/*koran*, which is

---

[42] Exodus 34:27-29 [NAB].

translated as *he-was-radiant*.⁴³ *The Englishman's Hebrew and Chaldee Concordance* informs us that קָרַן/*koran* can mean "**shine** or **to have horns,**"⁴⁴ like the horns of an ox or bull.

The 69th Psalm verse 31 also contains the word קֶרֶן/*koran*:

> **This also shall please the Lord better than an ox or bullock that hath horns and hoofs.**⁴⁵

When we read Psalm 69 in the original Hebrew, we again find the word קֶרֶן/*koran*.⁴⁶ The Bible translators have created a list of 67 phrases to translate the Hebrew word קֶרֶן/*koran*.

In his translation, **HAAK** includes the explanation for Moses being depicted with horns. When St. Jerome wrote the *Vulgate Bible*, he translated the original Hebrew into Latin. St. Jerome was the first translator to write Moses was horned; which may be linguistically correct, but certainly is **NOT** psychically correct!

When a person fasts for a long period of time, the connection between the physical body and the spiritual body becomes temporarily weakened. Under these conditions, a person can experience improved communication with the Spirit World. Many mediums of the Bible often fasted for long periods of time.

The *aura* is an energy light field that emanates from a person's soul. People with clairvoyant vision are able to see

---

⁴³ Kohlenberger, John R., III. *The NIV Interlinear Hebrew-English Old Testament. Vol. 1. Genesis – Deuteronomy.* Grand Rapids, MI: Zondervan, 1980. p. 246.
⁴⁴ *The Englishman's Hebrew and Chaldee Concordance of the Old Testament. Vol. 2.* London: Walton and Maberrly, 1866. p. 1439.
⁴⁵ Psalm 69:31 [KJV].
⁴⁶ Kohlenberger, John R., III. *The NIV Interlinear Hebrew-English Old Testament. Vol. 3. 1 Chronicles – Song of Songs.* Grand Rapids, MI: Zondervan, 1982. p. 421.

What Did Moses See at the Burning Bush?

and describe the aura, and its colors indicate a person's thoughts, personality, and emotions.

Moses fasted during the 40 days he spent on Mount Sinai, and in Spirit's presence. This intense experience caused Moses' aura to fully expand and his crown charka opened completely. A person who had clairvoyant vision would now see Moses' crown charka as a cone of light projected from the top of Moses' head.

Since the perimeter of the crown charka appears a bit thicker than the rest of it, some people thought the rays of light were coming out of Moses' head, which resembled horns of light.

When Moses came down the mountain, Moses' aura was so intense even people who did not have clairvoyant vision could detect its radiance. An experience such as this would be so great, that it would show through Moses' facial features for several days.

This is the reason St Jerome's mistranslated the Hebrew word קָרַן/*Koran* in the Vulgate Bible and Michelangelo had sculpt horns on his statue of Moses.

The ramification of Jerome's mistranslation has lasted for centuries, and became a source that infused anti-Semitism into people's minds.

In the 1970's, a Jewish friend of mine decided to attend Perdue University to earn her Master's Degree. One day, a group of mid-western Christian girls came up to my friend and asked her if she wouldn't mind showing them her horns! My friend was horrified that anyone living in the 20th century would still believe Jews had horns.

Understanding Moses' Horns

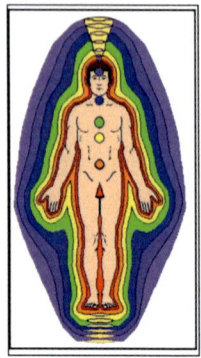  

1. When the auric field is fully opened and expanded, as Moses' was after spending 40 days on Mount Sinai with Spirit, a cone shape light emanates from the crown charka.

2. When looking directly at the person, the outer side edges of the cone appear denser or brighter then the rest of the cone.

3. The rays of light could resemble horns. However, Jerome inserted the word into his Vulgate Bible.

(kaw-ran') קָרַן
In KJV 4 times
Shine
1. Exodus 34:29 the skin of his face shone
2. Exodus 34:30 the skin of his face shone
3. Exodus 34:35 the skin of Moses face shone

Has Horns
1. Psalms 69:31 bullock that hath horns

And he knew not that his face was *horned* by the conversation of the talk of our Lord.
Exodus 34: 29 DOU

Woodcut from the great Cologne Bible of 1478. [James Strachan. *Pictures from a Mediaeval Bible*. Boston: Beacon Press, 1959. p. 55. Illus. # 41.

The Well of Moses by Claus Sluter, 1395–1403, Carthusian monastery of Chartreuse de Champmol built as a burial site by the Burgundian Duke Philip the Bold, Dijon, now France.
http://www.whale.to/c/moses.html July 26, 2014

Lladro Ten Commandments #5933 Sculptor: Salvador Furió Production Years: 1993-1996

MOSES UNIQUE AMONG THE PROPHETS

We are told Moses was unique among the prophets, because he was the only prophet to see God "face to face."

> Since then, no prophet has risen in Israel like Moses, whom the Lord knew face to face who did all those miraculous signs and wonders the Lord sent him to do in Egypt...."[47]

Yet, the Bible is full of contradictions, offering conflicting opinions about whether or not a human is able to see God and survive the experience. The New Testament makes a very clear and definitive statement that no one can see God.

> No one has seen God at any time.[48]

However, when we read the Bible story of Jacob wrestling an angel (Genesis 32: 24-32), we find this verse:

> Jacob named the place Peniel — "Face of God — "because I have seen God face to face, yet my life was spared."[49]

This story is very confusing because we are told Jacob wrestled a *man* (literally translated from the Hebrew), and suddenly this man was an angel or God? The reason for this shift remains unclear.

When Moses asked to see God's "glory" in Exodus 33:18, he is told that he would not survive seeing God's face.

> But, my face, he said, you can not see; mortal man cannot see me, and live to tell

---

[47] Deuteronomy 34: 10-11 [NIV].
[48] 1 John 04:12 [NASB].
[49] Genesis 32:30 [INCP].

of it.⁵⁰

Yet, the translator of **LIVT** uses alternative wording for this exact verse that has interesting implications.

> [God then] explained, "You cannot have a vision of My Presence. A man cannot have a vision of Me and still exist."⁵¹

LIVT claims *no one* can have *a vision of God*. This would include *seeing God with your physical eyes*, as **RKB** implied, and also include mediums/prophets having a clairvoyant vision of God, in their mind's eye. Yet **HIRS** contradicted **LIVT** when it informs us that another medium, Abraham saw God at אֵלוֹן מוֹרֶה /*Alon Moreh*:

> There God became visible to Abram and said....⁵²

An argument can be made to support the claim Abraham clairvoyantly saw God, or Abraham saw God materialize, just as Moses saw God materialize in the Meeting Tent.⁵³

We have a "plate of spaghetti" of intertwined, conflicting facts, which we may never untangle. These verses may disturb people who believe the Bible is a perfect document, without error or contradiction, and was dictated directly from God. There are obvious contradictions among these verses.

Yet, I conclude Moses never saw God at the Burning Bush. He never saw God directly, while he lived in his physical body. He did see God "face to face," when God

---

⁵⁰ Exodus 33:20 [RKB].
⁵¹ Exodus 33:20 [LIVT].
⁵² Gen. 12:7 [HIRS].
⁵³ See Schwartz, Sidney: *How Did Abraham See God?: The Bible as Psychic History*. Soon to be published.

entered the pillar of cloud (ectoplasm) in the Meeting Tent. God materialized in Moses' presence, and spoke to the physical people, who witnessed this event, to settle the people's disputes, answer their questions, and provide them guidance.

Spiritualists are accustomed to receive guidance and knowledge from Spirit. It is heart-breaking this living source of spiritual knowledge is not available to more people. Theologians of orthodox religions have steered their followers away from Spirit communication in order to keep their control over the masses of people.

This book once again demonstrates how Bible translators writing about psychically gifted people, we know as mediums, keep making errors in their Bible translations because they are ignorant of the *Gifts of the Spirit*. How different it would be, if all Christians had obeyed the directive of their founder, St. Paul, when he clearly stated:

> **"Fellow Christians, I want you to know about the gifts of the Spirit."**[54]

---

[54] 1 Corinthians 12:1 [BECK].

Bibliography

Bibles in Alphabetical Order

Abrev.	Date	Bible Citation
ABDNT	2002	Alexander, Victor N. *Aramaic Bible: Disciples New Testament*.
AEB	2001	*An American English Bible*.
ARAON	1982	Aberbach, Moses, and Grossfeld, Bernard. *Targum Onkelos to Genesis*.
ASV	1901	Schaff, Philip. *[American Standard Version]. The Holy Bible*.
BATE	1773	Bate, Julius. *A New & Literal Translation from the Original Hebrew of the Pentateuch of Moses*.
BECK	1976	Beck, William F. *The Holy Bible in the Language of Today*.
COV	1535	Coverdale, Miles. *The Bible*.
ETHJ	1862	Etheridge, John Wesley. *The Targums of Onkelos and Jonathan Ben Uzziël*.
GEDD	1792	Geddes, Alexander. *The Holy Bible*.
HIRS	1982	Hirsch, Samson Raphael. *The Pentateuch*.
HLYNB	1963	Traina, A. B., Rev. *The Holy Name Bible*.
HORNS	1911	Horner, George. *Coptic Version of the New Testament in the Southern Dialect*.
INCP	2007	*The Inclusive Bible: The First Egalitarian Translation*.
KJV	1611	*Authorized King James Version*.
LIV	1971	*The Living Bible: Paraphrased*.
LIVT	1981	Kaplan, Aryeh. *The Living Torah: The Five Books of Moses*.
NAB	1970	Catholic Biblical Association of America. *The New American Bible*.
NASB	1960	Lockman Foundation. *New American Standard Bible*.
NIrV	1996	*New International Reader's Version*.
NIV	1978	*[New International Version]. The Holy Bible*.
NLT	1996	*Holy Bible: New Living Translation*.
OANT	2009	Bauscher, Glenn David. *The Original Aramaic New Testament in Plain English*.
OGD	1950	Ogden, C. K. *The Basic Bible: Containing the Old & N.T. in Basic English*.
RKB	2009	Burke, Cormac. *Revised Knox Bible*.
RSV	1952	*[Revised Standard Version]. The Holy Bible*.
TEV	1976	*[Today's English Version]. Good News Bible: The Bible in Today's English*.

ABOUT THE AUTHOR
Sidney Schwartz

Rev. Sidney Schwartz earned a Bachelor's degree in history from the University of Bridgeport, and a Master's degree in educational media from Boston University. He resides in New Jersey, and is a retired middle school history teacher and school librarian. Rev. Schwartz studied mediumship for 37 years; and was ordained on February 25, 2001. He served as Assistant Pastor of Gifts of the Spirit Church. He became Pastor after its founder, Rev. Carl R. Hewitt, transitioned to the Spirit World.

It was in 2006 that Rev. Schwartz began his own mediumistic development by attending classes at the Arthur Findlay College (of Mediumship) in Stansted, England, where he took numerous classes in trance and platform mediumship. He has studied with mediums in New York metropolitan area.

In the 1970's his college friend, Bonnie Corwin-Hollis, introduced him to Rev. Carl Hewitt, a clairvoyant medium. During his first mediumistic reading, Rev. Hewitt had knowledge of his future and past, and provided specific details that no one else knew.

Several years later, Mr. Schwartz was summoned to Rev. Hewitt's office, because a Spirit entity wished to speak with him. Rev. Hewitt went to a trance state, and Mr. Schwartz had his first conversation with a powerful spirit entity, who refused to reveal his true identity. The angel explained that previously people who spoke with angels had created new religions. Since he did not wish to be the inspiration for still another religion, he would not reveal his identity, and would be addressed as AWAN, an acronym for **A**ngel **W**ithout **A** **N**ame.

From their first conversation, AWAN challenged Mr. Schwartz's religious beliefs, dropping a "bomb" in the form of an enraging and perplexing statement: "Catholic theologians repeatedly edited and changed the text of the Bible." Mr. Schwartz adamantly refused to believe anyone had altered the Torah. AWAN challenged him to use his research skills as a librarian and examine early Bible editions, to disprove his statement.

After intense study, Mr. Schwartz discovered AWAN's theory to be correct. To date, Rev. Schwartz has examined four hundred sixty-one versions of the Bible. When he compared the identical verse from these Bibles, he discovered the meaning varied radically, from translation to translation.

AWAN asked Mr. Schwartz to become his scribe, and write books of his teachings. Like Moses, Mr. Schwartz argued, because he lacked the confidence for this task. Eventually, he agreed, and wrote a trilogy of AWAN'S teachings. Crossovers: The Origin of Homosexuality Revealed is a companion book to the trilogy.

OTHER BOOKS

My First Encounter with an Angel

My First Encounter with an Angel is the first book of the Revelations of Ancient Wisdom - AWAN Speaks series. This trilogy will illuminate truths about how spirituality, mediumship, and prophecy have been hidden for centuries by Biblical translators and religious rulers. **AWAN**, the **A**ngel **W**ithout **A** **N**ame contacted the author, Sidney Schwartz, through the person of Carl Hewitt, a well-known trance medium. Who or what AWAN is does not ultimately matter as you read and examine the incredible information this sagacious Entity teaches.

AWAN revealed to the author during their first encounter, information about deliberate changes and alterations made in the Bible, throughout the centuries Church Fathers in order to suppress the psychic/spiritual development of their churchgoers. The author however, remained theologically adamant and argued with this angel. It was then that AWAN challenged the author to disprove his teachings. Using his skills as a librarian, the author researched extensively, studying over 160 versions of the Bible, only to discover that the AWAN taught the truth! Upon reading this book, you will begin to see the Bible is saturated with metaphysical or mediumistic phenomena of every kind.

BY SIDNEY SCHWARTZ & REV. CARL R. HEWITT

My Second Encounter with an Angel

In the late 1980's a well-known trance medium Rev. Carl R. Hewitt summonsed the author, Sidney Schwartz to his office. Carl entered a deep trance state, and **AWAN**, the **A**ngel **W**ithout **A N**ame, began speaking. Thus began a series of dialogs, in which AWAN imparted a large body of teachings.

My Second Encounter with an Angel contains the core of these teachings: explaining the power of human soul, and how one can reconnect with the God-within oneself. This book also explores long-forgotten psychic meanings behind the many religious rituals surrounding Palm Sunday, Ash Wednesday, Passover and Sukkot, as well as Spirit's perspective on the controversial social issues of suicide, abortion, and euthanasia.

AWAN insisted his theories should not automatically be accepted, but the author must think and reason the theories out against his own belief system. As a result, the author braided three separate strands to form this book. The *first strand* was the conversations the author had with AWAN. The *second strand* was corroborating historical evidence that supported AWAN's unusual theories. The *third strand* was various Bible verses, which either recorded psychic events, or were examples of the laws and rules the priests had inserted into the Bible.

My Third Encounter with an Angel

My Third Encounter with an Angel is the final book of the trilogy and brings Awan's teachings full circle. Awan's first teaching thoroughly disturbed the author: "Religious leaders have altered the Bible for their own purposes. They have inserted laws into the book and claimed they were God's laws. Priests wanted these laws in place to create fear and to control the masses." In this book, the author provides corroborating evidence, which completely proves Awan's statement.

It was important to Awan that he unbraided history to reveal the origin of homosexuality. Awan wanted to prove homosexuality is *not* a choice, and explained why some people are born gay. Once again, the author was able to find evidence, which proved Awan's controversial theory.

My Third Encounter with an Angel also examines how Christianity began as a religion of peace, which practiced mediumship during its church services, then morphed into a religion of suppression and extreme violence. Along its journey to become the only religion in Europe, Christians persecuted four groups of people. During the Late Middle Ages, these groups were braided together, tortured and finally executed. Women were branded as witches, male mediums branded as homosexuals, and/or Satanists. Jews were braided in with these groups and all of them were burned alive at the stake. The Church wrote doctrine after doctrine, which eventually made the distinctions between women, homosexuals, mediums and Jews invisible. This braid of destiny has caused these groups to be the scourge of western society, and vestiges of this animosity still exist today.

Throughout this trilogy Awan encouraged the author, and thereby the reader to think about his teachings, reason it out, and thus create your very own knowingness.

What Did Moses See at the Burning Bush?

Crossovers: The Origins of Homosexuality Revealed

True understanding of the reasons why certain people are homosexual is more important now than ever. Gay people are now fighting for their rights to enter into matrimonial relationships and to become parents. Providing answers to why religions, and society as a whole, have been homophobic for centuries; *"Crossovers: The Origins of Homosexuality* is not only a long overdue history lesson, but may also help to reunite families who have been tom apart by bias and a lack of understanding.

Carl Hewitt, the widely acclaimed medium, was at times been referred to as a modern-day Nostradamus. Although he never advertised, his clients traveled to his office from all over the United States, and abroad. Carl frequently shared critical information from his psychical visions with the FBI. This began before the attempted assassination of President Reagan, through the aftermath of 9/11.

On March 16, 1978, an ascended spiritual master, the **A**ngel **W**ithout **A N**ame (AWAN) spoke with Carl for the first time. Throughout the 1990's Awan spoke through Carl's entranced body, on a regular basis, to convey a body of teachings. Sidney Schwartz, a middle school librarian from Hackensack, New Jersey was chosen to hear these teachings, transcribe them into a book, after verifying the historical information with research.

This book chronicles Rick's journey from rejecting to accepting his own homosexuality. Rick last step before committing suicide, was to seek counseling from Rev. Carl Hewitt. Awan intervened and offered to teach Rick the origin of homosexuality and the reason for religions' homophobic attitudes, provided that Sidney Schwartz was present to record and document these sessions. The author literally found the verification of Awan's explanation of the origin of homosexuality carved in stone.

The Golden Thread: Mediumship in the Bible

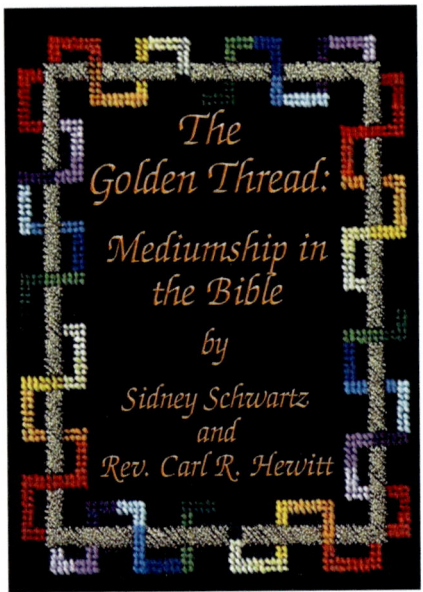

If all of history were a tapestry of time, a *Golden Thread* would be woven throughout, symbolizing the working of Spirit. This *Golden Thread* is contrasted against a dark background of ignorance, that theologians perpetuated to keep the truth of the Spirit World hidden from humanity.

The Golden Thread will examine history from a new perspective, through the eyes of a medium. The aim of this book is to explain the workings of Spirit, known today as parapsychology or psychic phenomena and to relate this phenomena with historical events, to demonstrate how mankind has been guided by Spirit since the beginning of time. The presentation of alternative theories is not intended to convert the reader's beliefs, but to provide rational evidence to support and enhance the reader's convictions.

Most of the major personalities of the Bible were mediums, and demonstrated at least one of the *Gifts of the Spirit*. *The Golden Thread* will explain how each of the *Gifts of the Spirit* functions and clarify which Biblical medium demonstrated that gift. The laws of psychic science have never changed, and what was true in Biblical times, is still true today.

The text of the Bible has filtered through the minds of hundreds of translators, and as a result many translations have been infused with translators' biases and agendas not found in in the original texts. Despite the fact there are over 500 translations of the Bible, much psychic meaning and information is embedded in the original Hebrew of the Old Testament, which is never included in English translations.

What Did Moses See at the Burning Bush? 41
The Bible as Psychic History: An Overview

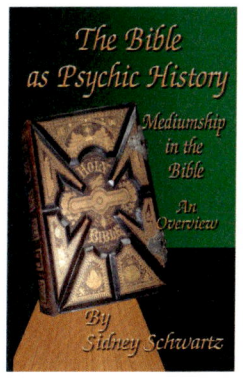

The great majority of Bible personalities were mediums. They heard the voice of God and saw divine visions. The study the mediumship and psychic phenomena within the text of the Holy Bible is a major task. It is not the purpose of this book to examine every mediumistic event found in the Bible; but to provide the reader a basic understanding of this vast subject. Although many books have been written about mediumship in the Bible, this book is unique. *The Bible as Psychic History* begins to unearth additional layers of psychic information embedded in the original Hebrew of the Old Testament. Most Bible translators ignored this layer because they were not educated in psychic science. They do not understand nor recognize the significance of this evidence, which proves the theory — the Bible is indeed a book of psychic history.

How I Survived the Holocaust: Rita Teper Schwartz's Story

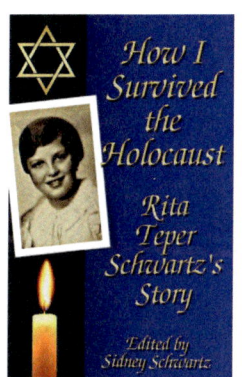

Hitler's Nazi troops marched into Rita Teper's hometown of Vienna, Austria. Immediately, her life changed and this young girl repeatedly found herself confronting adult, life-threatening situations. The story of Rita's family's escape from the Nazis' murderous clutches has more twist and turns than a modern-day soap opera. This narrative describes her harrowing journey smuggling across the Belgian border, where her family had to wait 18 months for papers to immigrate to the United States. They received these papers just as Hitler was to invade Belgium. This book not only talks about Rita Teper Schwartz's immediate family, but discusses her extended family as well. Some traveled to safety to the United States, while the Nazis murdered others, and one managed to survive internment in two concentration camps. Pictures and a family tree of her extended family are included, as well as government issued documents: such as a work permit, passport, several identification cards, a U. S. immigration identification card and citizenship papers. This book is not only a glimpse of one family's terror and suffering inflicted by the cruelty of Nazi oppression; but is also an inspiring story of escape and survival.

FURTHER INFORMATION
Gifts of the Spirit Church

To learn more about
Gifts of the Spirit Church,
please visit our website:
www.gotsc.org

Made in the USA
Middletown, DE
01 May 2019